UNSOLVED QUESTIONS ABOUT EARTH

BY MYRA FAYE TURNER

CAPSTONE PRESS
a capstone imprint

Published by Capstone Press, an imprint of Capstone
1710 Roe Crest Drive
North Mankato, Minnesota 56003
capstonepub.com

Library of Congress Cataloging-in-Publication Data is available on the Library of Congress website

ISBN: 9781669002529 (hardcover)
ISBN: 9781669002475 (paperback)
ISBN: 9781669002482 (ebook PDF)

Summary: How did Earth form? Where did all the water come from? How did Earth's plates begin to shift? When it comes to our planet, there are a whole lot of questions we're still trying to answer. Get ready to explore the unknown and discover how scientists are working to solve the mysteries of Earth.

Editorial Credits
Editor: Christopher Harbo; Designer: Sarah Bennett; Media Researcher: Svetlana Zhurkin; Production Specialist: Katy LaVigne

Image Credits
Alamy: Bluegreen Pictures, 25; Getty Images: Douglas Peebles, 13, Jiraporn Meereewee, 15, Rainer von Brandis, 4, Ralph White, 22, Science Photo Library/Mark Garlick, 8, 21, Science Photo Library/Roger Harris, 20, Stocktrek Images/Frieso Hoevelkamp, 16–17, Vince Streano, 29; Shutterstock: Aphelleon, cover (top), atanasis (background), cover and throughout, beboy, 11, Designua, 10, 24, Dr Project (background), cover and throughout, fboudrias, cover (bottom right), JBArt, 9, Kolonko, 12, Mopic, 6–7, Natalia Lukiyanova Frenta, 27, Petr Salinger, cover (bottom left), Rainer Lesniewski, 23, Sandra Cunningham, 14, VectorMine, 28, Warpaint, cover (bottom middle), 19

TABLE OF CONTENTS

Words in **bold** are in the glossary.

OUR MYSTERIOUS PLANET

Earth is our home, but it's still a place of mystery. Luckily, we have curious scientists. They help us understand our world. Geologists study Earth's surface and what it's made of. Marine biologists study our oceans. Astronomers study how Earth came to be. Archaeologists look back in time to study human and animal life.

| A marine biologist uses an underwater writing device to record notes about a coral reef.

One of Earth's biggest mysteries is its age. Scientists believe the third planet from the sun is about 4.6 billion years old. Many more mysteries remain unsolved. Where did all our water come from? Why did the dinosaurs die out? What's at the bottom of the ocean? Get ready to explore these and other questions about Earth.

THE SCIENTIFIC METHOD

Scientists use a process called the scientific method to answer unsolved questions about our planet. They follow these steps:

- Ask a question
- Gather information
- Make a prediction
- Design an experiment to test the question
- Collect data
- Analyze data
- Draw conclusions
- Communicate results

CHAPTER 1

HOW DID EARTH FORM?

Imagine traveling back in time to when our planet formed. What would you see? Our home likely began as a cloud of dust and gas. So it would look very different than it does today.

Today, Earth has a rocky surface. But scientists aren't sure how our planet formed. One belief is a distant star caved in and created an explosion of swirling clouds. These clouds—known as a **solar nebula**—spun out of control. This motion caused the dust and gas to stick together. These clumps may have formed all of the planets in our solar system, including Earth.

FACT Earth may have formed in a solar nebula billions of years ago. But our planet's name, which means "the ground," is only about 1,000 years old.

| Earth and the moon were red-hot balls of rock when they
first formed about 4.6 billion years ago.

Over time, our planet changed. At first Earth was
very hot. Melted rocks dotted the landscape. But at
some point, after millions of years, it cooled down.
This allowed deep blue oceans to form. Then different
layers of the planet developed.

Earth continued changing. The land reshaped.
Grand rocky mountains reached for the sky. Deep
valleys dipped into the ground. Vast flat plains
stretched far and wide. The movement of icy **glaciers**
and eruptions of blazing-hot volcanoes also helped
form planet Earth.

THE GOLDILOCKS PLANET

Earth is sometimes called the Goldilocks planet. It's not too hot or too cold. As the planet evolved, gases wrapped around Earth, creating our **atmosphere**. This blanket of oxygen and other elements makes it possible for Earth to support plants, animals, and humans.

| Earth is just the right distance from the sun to support life.

CHAPTER 2

WHEN AND HOW DID EARTH'S PLATES BEGIN MOVING?

Today, Earth has seven **continents**. But it was once one big island. That island was called Pangaea. Over time, the island split and formed our continents.

What do you see when you look at a picture of Earth from space? It looks like a giant jigsaw puzzle! In some ways it is. Earth's continents, which sit on huge tectonic plates, would fit together if they were smooshed up against each other.

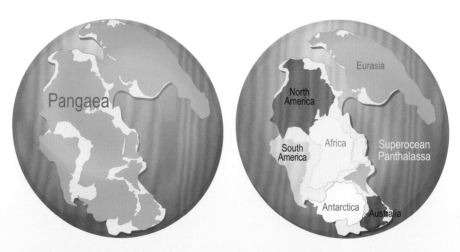

| The huge island of Pangaea broke apart to create the continents we know today.

Earth's plates are always moving. They move slowly. They move about 1 to 2 inches (2.5 to 5 centimeters) a year. That's about as long as a paperclip.

Sometimes the plates pull apart. Other times they squeeze together. What is the result? Exploding volcanoes and rumbling earthquakes.

| Most of Earth's volcanoes have formed along the edges of the planet's tectonic plates.

FACT Scientists have a name for the movement of Earth's plates. It's called plate tectonics.

The study of Earth's plates dates back more than 100 years. But scientists still don't know when or how the plates started moving. One reason for the mystery is simple. Not much of Earth's early surface is around to study.

The plates may have started moving 1 billion years ago. Or around 3 billion years ago. They may have even begun to drift apart less than a billion years ago. Scientists don't know for sure.

Could heat have caused one large plate to break into smaller ones? That's one belief. It's very hot beneath Earth's outer layer. It was even hotter billions of years ago. It's possible blazing hot temperatures made the plates easier to shift.

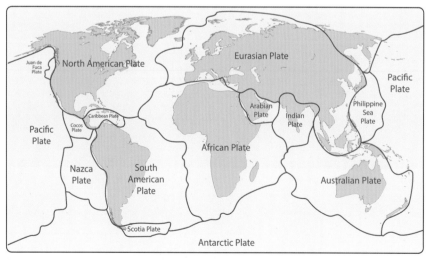

| Most of Earth's tectonic plates meet deep below the oceans.

Scientists may one day figure out when Earth's plates began moving. But the science of why they started moving is likely to remain a mystery.

CAN SCIENTISTS PREDICT EARTHQUAKES?

The shifting of Earth's plates can cause cracks, or fault lines. When two plates rub against each other along these cracks, they cause an earthquake. Scientists know *how* earthquakes happen. They can even predict which areas might be hit. But *when* an earthquake will happen can't be predicted.

| Scientists study cracks along Earth's tectonic plates to better understand earthquakes and volcanoes.

CHAPTER 3

WHERE DID EARTH'S WATER COME FROM?

Our planet is sometimes called "the blue planet." That's because much of Earth's surface is covered in water. In fact, about 71 percent of our planet is covered by water. Water exists in clear lakes, muddy rivers, icy glaciers, and deep, blue oceans.

— THE WATER CYCLE —

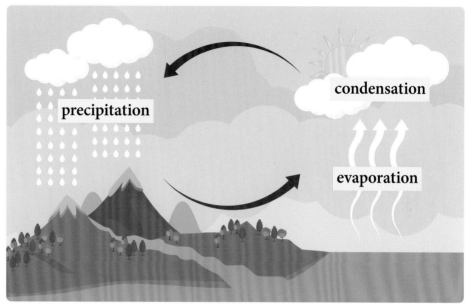

| The three main stages of the water cycle are evaporation, condensation, and precipitation.

As far as we know, Earth is the only planet that has liquid water. The water we drink today has been on Earth for billions of years. How is that possible? It has been recycled in a process called the water cycle. The water cycle begins in our oceans and lakes. Water **evaporates** into a vapor that floats up and forms the clouds. Then it **condenses** and falls back to Earth as **precipitation**, such as rain and snow. The process then starts all over again.

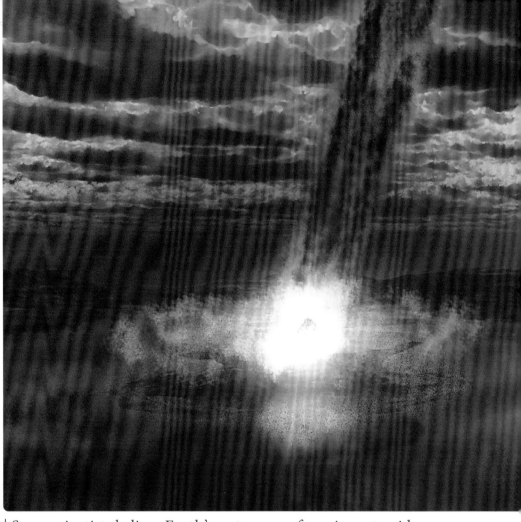

| Some scientists believe Earth's water came from icy asteroids and comets that crashed onto the planet.

Earth's water has always been here, but where did it come from? Scientists aren't sure.

One belief is giant ice-filled **asteroids** or **comets** brought water to Earth. The water didn't arrive in one trip. These space rocks rained down on Earth over time. In fact, it may have happened over millions of years.

Some scientists believe our water supply was created when Earth formed. Others disagree. They see a problem with this idea. Earth was boiling hot and didn't have an atmosphere when it formed. Some scientists think any water during this time would have gone back into space.

It's possible Earth's water came from both sources. But it's a mystery scientists may never completely solve.

CHAPTER 4

WHY DID ALL THE DINOSAURS DIE OUT?

Dinosaurs ruled the planet for more than 160 million years. Then, for some reason, they disappeared about 66 million years ago. Could smaller animals have eaten the dinosaurs' eggs, causing them to die out? Did disease wipe them out? Probably not, scientists say.

One reason dinosaurs may have vanished from Earth is climate change. Just before the dinosaurs disappeared, the temperature of the planet plunged. It's possible volcanic eruptions filled the air with smoke and ash. This debris would have blocked the sun, causing Earth to cool down. Because dinosaurs were cold-blooded, they needed sunlight to heat their bodies to survive.

But some scientists disagree. They say climate change would have taken a long time. Dinosaurs would probably have adapted to the changes.

| The mighty *Tyrannosaurus rex* lived on Earth during the end of the Cretaceous period, roughly 85 to 65 million years ago.

| Some scientists believe a massive meteorite may have crashed onto Earth and doomed the dinosaurs.

Another idea is a giant **meteorite** hit Earth and killed all the dinosaurs. Scientists say a crater found in 1991 in Mexico proves it. They believe the meteorite caused earthquakes, volcanic eruptions, wildfires, and **tsunamis**. Some dinosaurs and many other animals and plants would have died during these events.

FACT British scientist Sir Richard Owen coined the word *dinosaur* in 1842. He was the first scientist to say dinosaurs were a different species than other reptiles.

As for the rest, the years of darkness and freezing temperatures that followed may have spelled their doom. Plants withered and died. Without a food source, plant-eating dinosaurs starved. Then the meat-eating dinosaurs eventually died out, too, without a steady source of food.

However, some scientists still aren't convinced. A meteorite impact doesn't explain why many other plants and animals from that time still survived. Since there's no definite proof, for now, this mystery remains unsolved.

| Volcanic debris caused by a meteorite strike may have blocked out sunlight, making Earth too cold for dinosaurs to survive.

CHAPTER 5

WHAT LIVES IN THE DEEPEST PARTS OF THE OCEAN?

One of the most mysterious places on Earth is the bottom of the ocean. As of 2021, scientists have explored only about 20 percent of this huge undersea world. It seems like it would be easy to just dive down and take a peek. But it's not.

| Scientists use submersibles to explore some of the deepest parts of the ocean.

Many parts of the ocean are thousands of feet deep. For this reason, explorers must use deep-sea **submersibles** to travel below the surface. When divers are outside these vessels, they need scuba gear to help them breathe while exploring.

But exploring the ocean floor is challenging. The deeper you go, the harder it is to breathe—even with special equipment. At extreme depths, the pressure of the water pushing down on you is crushing. It would feel like an elephant sitting on your chest!

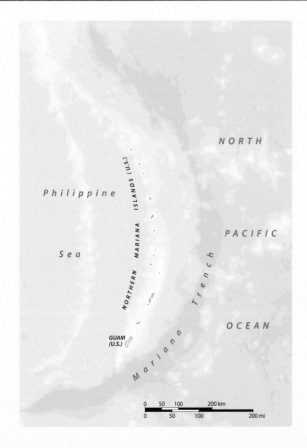

THE MARIANA TRENCH

The deepest part of the ocean is the Mariana Trench. The trench is located in the Pacific Ocean, near Guam and the Mariana Islands. To reach the bottom, you would need to go down 36,201 feet (11,034 meters). That's about 7 miles (11 kilometers)! Only three people have explored the Mariana Trench. Scientists Jacques Piccard and Donald Walsh made the first trip in 1960. Movie director James Cameron went there in 2012.

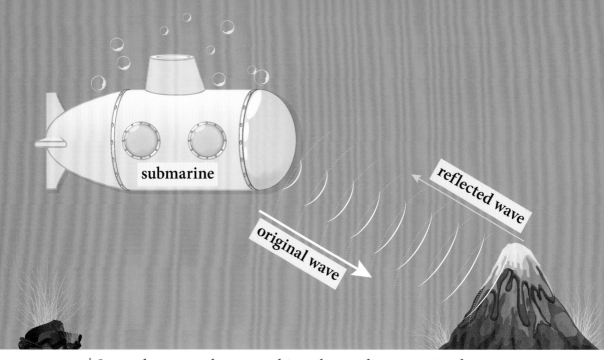

Sonar detects underwater objects by sending out sound waves and measuring how long it takes them to reflect back.

In addition to the pressure, no sunlight reaches the deepest parts of the oceans. It's impossible to see anything without artificial light. So how do scientists explore the ocean floor? They use sonar and remote-controlled vehicles. Sonar bounces sound waves off underwater objects to detect their location, size, and shape. Remote-controlled vehicles allow scientists to take pictures and videos of what's on the ocean floor.

FACT Divers can swim down about 60 feet (18.2 m) without using special gear. That's about the same distance from the ground to the top of a 6-story building.

Over the years, scientists have discovered many strange sea creatures living at the bottom of the ocean. The anglerfish is one of them. These weird-looking fish have a thread growing out of their heads, which they use like a fishing lure. When the tip of the thread glows, small fish are drawn to the light. Then chomp! The anglerfish gobbles them up with its sharp teeth.

| The light in an anglerfish's lure is produced by millions of bacteria inside its tip.

Still, most of the world's oceans remain unexplored. Who knows what other mysterious creatures might be lurking down there?

CHAPTER 6

WHAT LIES AT THE CENTER OF EARTH?

Imagine digging to the center of Earth. What do you think you would find? The center of Earth is blazing hot. So all we can do is guess what might be there.

What scientists do know is Earth has four layers. The first layer is called the crust. It's the cool outer layer of dirt and rocks under your feet. The next layer is called the mantle. This layer is mostly hot, solid rock. Then there's the outer core. This third layer is made of liquid iron and nickel. It looks like gooey melted caramel.

Earth's last layer is called the inner core. It is thousands of miles beneath the crust, at the very center of Earth. The temperature of the core is between 7,900 and 10,800 degrees Fahrenheit (4,370 to 5,980 degrees Celsius). Standing near the core would be like standing next to the sun!

— EARTH'S LAYERS —

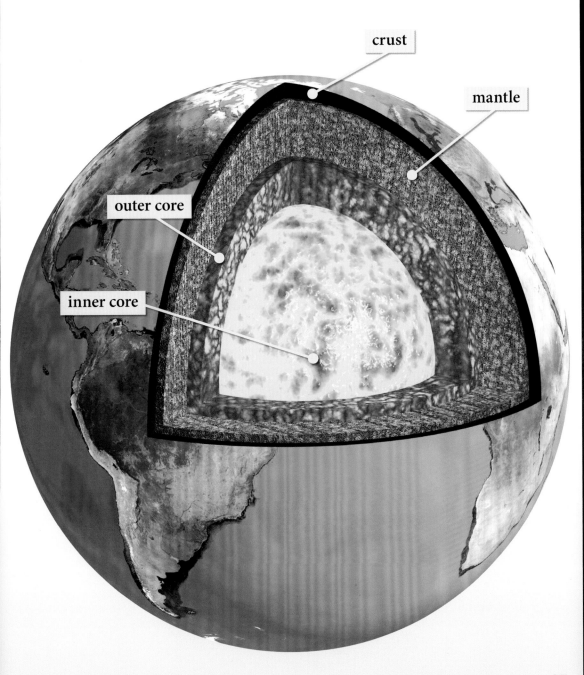

crust

mantle

outer core

inner core

Earth's core is too deep and hot for scientists to visit. Instead, they have to depend on other ways to learn about the center of Earth. One way is by using information from the **seismic waves** of an earthquake. These waves travel through Earth's layers. Scientists know that primary waves can pass through both solids and liquids. But secondary waves can only pass through solids.

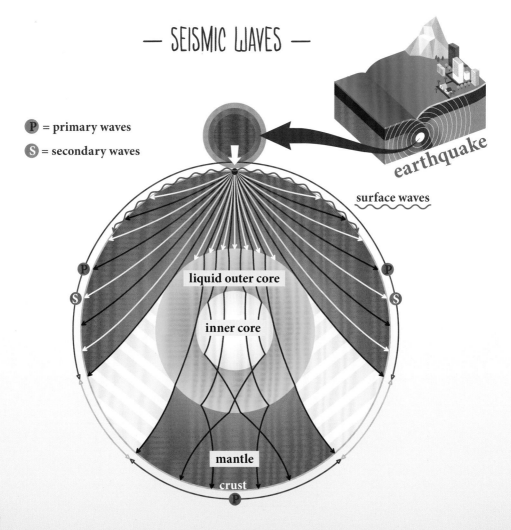

— SEISMIC WAVES —

P = primary waves

S = secondary waves

earthquake

surface waves

liquid outer core

inner core

mantle

crust

| A scientist studies the readings of a seismograph to understand the strength and duration of seismic waves.

Using seismic wave data, scientists believed for many years that Earth's inner core contained solid iron and nickel. But recent findings have left them unsure. A report published in 2022 suggests the core may not be solid. Instead, it may contain other, lighter elements. If that's true, it proves our planet's core will likely remain a mystery for many years to come.

From Earth's early formation to what lies deep in its core, our planet is still full of mysteries. Today, scientists don't have all the answers. But as they continue to learn, maybe one day they will.

FACT Russia's Kola Superdeep Borehole is the deepest hole ever dug. It extends about 7.5 miles (12 km) into Earth's surface. That's deeper than the Mariana Trench!

GLOSSARY

asteroid (AS-tuh-royd)—a large rock that travels through space

atmosphere (AT-muh-sfeer)—the mixture of gases that surrounds Earth

comet (KOM-uht)—a ball of rock and ice that circles the sun

condense (kuhn-DENS)—to change from gas to liquid; water vapor condenses into liquid water

continent (KAHN-tuh-nuhnt)—one of Earth's seven large land masses

evaporate (i-VA-puh-rayt)—to change from a liquid into a vapor or a gas

glacier (GLAY-shur)—a large, slow-moving sheet of ice found in mountain valleys or polar regions

meteorite (MEE-tee-uhr-ite)—a chunk of rock that hits a planet

precipitation (pri-sip-i-TAY-shuhn)—water that falls from the clouds in the form of rain, hail, or snow

seismic waves (SIZE-mik WAYVZ)—waves created by an earthquake

solar nebula (SOH-lur NEB-yoo-la)—huge clouds of gas and dust in space from which a solar system forms

submersible (sub-MURS-uh-buhl)—a small underwater craft powered by motors

tsunami (soo-NAH-mee)—gigantic ocean wave created by an undersea earthquake, landslide, or volcanic eruption

READ MORE

Armentrout, Patricia. *Our Amazing Earth*. New York: Crabtree Publishing Company, 2022.

Rake, Jody S. *Earth*. North Mankato, MN: Capstone, 2021.

Stewart-Sharpe, Leisa. *Our Blue Planet*. New York. Simon & Schuster Books for Young Readers, 2023.

INTERNET SITES

Nasa Science: Space Place
spaceplace.nasa.gov/all-about-earth/en

National Geographic Kids: Save the Earth
kids.nationalgeographic.com/nature/save-the-earth

The Nine Planets: Earth Facts for Kids
nineplanets.org/kids/earth

INDEX

ABOUT THE AUTHOR

Myra Faye Turner is a New Orleans-based poet and author. She has written for grown-ups, but prefers writing for young readers. She has written more than two dozen fiction and nonfiction books for children and young adults, covering diverse topics like politics, the Apollo moon landing, edible insects, Black history, U.S. history, and science. When she's not writing, she spends her days reading, napping, playing Wordle, and drinking coffee.